MW01174511

Masters of the Craft

Masters of the Craft

Don Gutteridge

Hidden Brook Press

First Edition

Hidden Brook Press
www.HiddenBrookPress.com
writers@HiddenBrookPress.com
EST. 1994

Masters of the Craft
by Don Gutteridge

Layout and Design – Richard M. Grove
Cover Design – Richard M. Grove
Cover Art – agsandrew, courtesy of Shutterstock.

Printed and bound in Canada

Library and Archives Canada Cataloguing in Publication

Title: Masters of the craft / Don Gutteridge.
Names: Gutteridge, Don, 1937- author.
Description: Poems.
Identifiers: Canadiana 20210278188 |
            ISBN 9781989786512 (softcover)
Classification: LCC PS8513.U85 M37 2021 |
            DDC C811/.54—dc23

The Anxiety of Influence:
reading Don Gutteridge's
Masters of the Craft"

There's nothing that makes a writer cringe like Harold
Bloom's phrase *the anxiety of influence* wherein the
central agony of all aspiring poets at the beginning of
their journey involves the idea that they are in
competition with their progenitors. Shakespeare set
the bar so high one might surrender in the womb
saying, "Why do I even bother?". And then there
comes the great borrowing. Al Purdy, Canada's
unofficial Poet Laureate in English for all time stole a
slight rewording of Cicero's phrase from the *Dream of
Scipio* calling his fourth book *The Craft so Long to Learn.*
One might be forgiven if scholarship begins with
Chaucer's use of the phrase "The Lyf so short, the
craft so long to Lerne," from his *Prologue to the Parliament
of Fowls*. What originated in Greek, was stolen by the
Latins, then by way of the literary larceny of Chaucer
came into English, and then eventually arrived in a
chapbook title by our own Al Purdy.

Who else to learn from but the great artists on
whose shoulders we stand? Why steal a wormy apple
when it sours the appetite and spoils the meal? I
suggest a writer should steal only the best and brightest

apples from the orchards of the Lord. And the question arises, 'what is the difference between anxiety and homage?' Surely there's a little bit of Shakespeare in every writer since the bard of Avon first took up the pen. The *Beatitudes* reveal themselves as originating with the Sermon on the Mount, and yet they too have their progenitors in ancient Egyptian texts. From Gilgamesh through Homer and from Homer to Shakespeare and from Shakespeare to some neophyte composing verses of teenage angst in a high school library somewhere in Frozen Lung Saskatchewan, it's reading that births the best of all writing. Of course, books are not born in libraries, and writers live in the world, but libraries are essential to the world in which writers live.

And so, in Don Gutteridge's series of poems *Masters of the Craft* we are gifted to receive a major poet's homage to some of his influences. These poems are written as though to open the window and let in the light. We see Emily Dickinson bending over the page and writing as though in intimate communication with an as of yet unborn lad from Point Edward by way of Sarnia. These poems give us the poet as a reader of poets. They are each and every one something of an invitation to common admiration. Who has not been awestruck by a line of prose in a Dickens' moment? Who has not experienced the frisson of pleasure, that taking-the-top-of-the-head off endorphin rush reading John Keats or Thomas Hardy?

In his recent essay world-renowned bibliophile Alberto Manguel writes, "My own imagination has been constantly fed by my library, which has been an unending source of insight into humanity." Reading Don Gutteridge's suite of poems in praise of a few of the poets and authors he most admires, I am reminded of the sacred duty of ancestor worship. I think of my own list of influences and know I have much common ground with the jewels in the crown of this major poet's literary coronal.

John B. Lee
Poet Laureate of the city of Brantford in perpetuity
Poet Laureate of Norfolk County for life
Poet Laureate of Canada Cuba Literary Alliance

Contents

Forward – The Anxiety of Influence – John B. Lee – *p. vii*
Author's Note – *p. 1*

– Emily – *p. 3*
– Dylan – *p. 5*
– Hardy – *p. 7*
– Emily – *p. 9*
– Keats – *p. 11*
– Keats, Again – *p. 13*
– Will – *p. 15*
– Shelley – *p. 17*
– Coleridge – *p. 19*
– Purdy – *p. 21*
– Acorn – *p. 23*
– Pratt – *p. 25*
– Layton – *p. 27*
– Dickens – *p. 29*
– Eliot – *p. 31*
– Twain – *p. 33*
– Lawrence – *p. 35*
– Hemingway – *p. 37*
– Homage – *p. 39*

Author Bio – *p. 41*

Masters of the Craft

Author's Note:

The tributes below are not meant to be a greatest hits list. I selected poets and novelists I have long admired, both from the English canon and from Canadian poets I have teethed on. The selection is very much personal and idiosyncratic. John B. Lee is the only living writer here. He has been called the greatest living poet in English and I believe he is Canada's best. I consider him to be a friend. Finally, I had to be certain, after selecting an author, that there was a poem waiting to be written. I am honoured in having John B. Lee add a preface to this collection.

Emily Dickinson
December 10, 1830 – May 15, 1886

Emily

You winched a world into
twelve rhymed lines
and molded metaphor out of
butterflies and bees
and told the ruthless truth
in semaphores and similes,
homespun or sublime,
and if the universe seemed
to roll on by, you turned
an eye, unflinching,
towards Eternity.

Dylan Thomas
October 27, 1914 – November 9, 1953

Dylan

Dylan! You wrote
with a bardic ardour, like a
Welsh troubadour peddling
ballads door-to-door,
like a boulevard busker performing
for pittance or pennies, and we loved
your raunchy rhymes, your muscular
rhythms and the Celtic tang
that sang in your chains like the sea,
and you must have been there
when there were wolves in Wales
and the fens were livid with light,
and we knew that you too
would not go gentle into
any Good Night.

Thomas Hardy
June 2, 1840 – January 11, 1928

Hardy

You penned novels to make
a buck, not knowing
that *Jude the Obscure* wouldn't be,
or that guileless girls everywhere
would find in *Tess* and the dark
arc of its narrative something
to unease, and that
the bad luck in *The Mayor,*
brokered by the Fates, would prompt
alarm in the Presbyterian
heart, and so too
do we have the poems, standing
in their own light, words
as chiselled as china, as sturdy
as star-struck Stonehenge. –

Emily Brontë
July 30, 1818 – December 19, 1848

Emily

You were a child of the moors,
of the wind-whetted, heather –
breathing heath, where Fancy
could dance to its own groomed
tune, and you let it
dream you a wild, wuthering
abode – with a master crafted
out of blood and granite,
and characters who quickened first
in those thumb-thick
tomes you and your siblings
drew out of your need to be,
and you never knew the world
would someday succumb
to the timeless truths of that
tubercular-tinged tale,
long after the slow erosion
of your half-lived life.

John Keats
October 31, 1795 – February 23, 1821

Keats

You celebrated urns and nightingales,
autumnal mists and La Belle
Dame in verses as distilled
as Grecian light, oozing
allusion and alliterative
lilt, and you had the gift
of a bard's gilded grammar
and the rigour of his rapturous rhyme,
as if the propagation of poems
alone could keep you alive
long enough to write
yourself out of words – before
the wasting disease vanished
your voice, and on the day
you died, bees in their hives
unhummed and in the woods
nearby, no birds sang

Keats, Again

Hummingbird Summer

It must be a hummingbird summer
because bees in their numberless
buzzing are brushing the bluebell
blooms with their lush bellies,
and roses on the arch of their arbour
sweeten in the sun, and in the field
beyond my window, once
fallow, winter wheat
thickens and sags, and redwings
nearby whistle a two –
note tune and their country
cousins sparrow the air
with their flocked fluttering,
and along the bone-white
side-road ragweed
ripens among the bull
thistle, and I dream of Keats
and his lonely odes: of nightingales
and Grecian crockery and Autumn's
mistfulness, uttering blood
to abide, and etch his poems
perpetual.

William Shakespeare
April 1564 – April 23, 1616

Will

When Will, the would-be bard
from Avon arrived at the Globe,
quill aquiver, and trod
the boards to make a shilling
or two, every time
he scribbled lines poetic,
they stammered iambic until
he let the syllables sing
in pulsing pentameters,
and the lexicon he lassoed
was still elastic, alive
with sturdy Saxon verbs
and nuanced nouns and upstart
pretenders from the Latin
and Greek he eschewed in school,
and he hammered out poems and plays
like a man bruised lucid
by the Muse and, with a nod
to the groundlings, liberated the language
from the grip of the privileged few
in their lofty loges – and made it
ours.

Percy Bysshe Shelley
August 4, 1792 – July 8, 1822

Shelley

You wept for Adonais
and all those poets
who kept the faith and faded
like Ozymandias in a
desert dream or Keats
killed by the critics for their sport,
but you were seized by something
living aloud within
and the poems poured forth
like the west wind wild
inside or the soaring symmetries
of the skylark or that
polysyllabic mouthful,
Epipsychidian where you plumbed
the dubious purviews of the demonic
and let them sing for themselves,
and then, waving farewell
to Mary and the Muses, you set
sail on Grecian seas
like Prometheus unbound,
and drowned.

Samuel Taylor Coleridge
October 21, 1772 – July 25, 1834

Coleridge

You smoked opium to stoke
the fires that burned in your brain,
where Poesy and Disquisition
resided in some unease
and occasionally coincided
to produce the dream-imbued
Kubla and his Pleasure Dome
or the sea-faring farrago
of an ancient mariner, and I can
still see you and William,
a brace of lyrical balladeers,
combing the Cumbrian hills
for that poem-potent tranquility
which is the bliss of solitude.

Al (Alfred Wellington) Purdy
December 30, 1918 – April 21, 2000

Purdy

He combed the nooks and crannies
of a country and a good bit
of the world for fodder to feed
the pulsing need of his poems,
this connoisseur of the commonplace,
this oracle of the ordinary,
this troubadour of the imprudent
who churned out muscular verse
by the baker's dozen, leavened
with a lyric lilt, wherein
home-made beer
and Caribou horses and all
the Annettes coexisted
in friendly felicity and an A-frame
was made famous – and when
he left us, his soul drifted
somewhere north of summer.

Milton James Rhode Acorn
March 30, 1923 – August 20, 1986

Acorn

You tasted your blood too much
to abide what you were born to,
your battered nose worn
like a buffoon's badge to un-
welcome the world, and no girl
ever called you handsome,
yet you composed poems
in both love and anger
like a passionate assassin,
like a ribald bride, like a
disbarred bard
in Jack-Pine sonnets
oozing assonance and rhymes
that ricocheted all the way
to the heart, where you live
still.

E. J. (Edwin John Dove) Pratt
February 4, 1882 – April 26, 1964

Pratt

He was both bibled and bibulous,
a man of the Good Book
and a groaning table, a sophisticate
of Dickens and tropes, but there was
always something of the Newfie
ticking within, the urge
to spin a yarn just
this side of the truth in long
loping lines on the lookout
for a rhyme, where cachalots did in
ten-tentacled squid,
and icebergs, calved
from the mother-lode,
halved the *Titanic* and watched
little children drown,
where muscular mollusks
and whiskered whelk weathered
the Darwinian dark,
and this soothsaying scrivener
penned epic after epic
of krakens awakening and Jesuits
in jeopardy – until the last
spike was driven.

Irving Peter Layton
March 12, 1912 – January 4, 2006

Layton

When your muse struck,
you switched on the erotic
throttle, but there was always
something more amorous
than sex-hectic in those
anthems to the joys of the
conjugal joust, more Eros
than Bacchanalian, and you were
born with the lyric lilt
and the natural knack you used
to immortalize Keine Lazarovitch,
and before all was said and done,
you laid down a red carpet
for the sun.

Charles Dickens
February 7, 1812 – June 9, 1870

Dickens

At first you dazzled London
with your Pickwickian picaresques
and then delved deeper
with portraits of a city's slum,
where ragamuffins and shoeless
paupers, benumbed by hunger
and chancred by cold, were winched
into warrens, where rats revived
and humans didn't, and there poured
from the majestic maelstrom of your mind
more than a dozen tales:
of Pip and David and Little
Nell and Sairy Gamp
with her plumped umbrella
and Mr. Micawber, forever
the odd-man out,
and the indebted denizens
of *Bleak House,* romancing
the Chancery, and Mr. Krook
who went up, unloved, in a puff
of smoke, and the hundred other
nicknamed cousins
we'll remember as long as there is
ink to print and the need
to read.

T. S. Eliot
September 26, 1888 – January 4, 1965

Eliot

When Prufrock with the bottom
of his trousers rolled, hit
the pristine pages of *Poetry*,
he shook the panjandrums
of verse down to the shiver
of their shoes, and you caught
in the lassitude of those lines
something of the malaise
of those derelict days
before the horrors of war
made the blood-beat
of ballads impossible, and then
you stunned us once again
when *The Waste Land* tore
its scorched-earth truths
across our complacencies,
unrhymed and rhythmic-raw,
and like Ludwig you bowed out
with late quartets, a brooding
fugue of sound and sense
that left "Little Gidding"
to illume our language, while the
women come and go,
talking of Michelangelo.

Mark Twain
November 30, 1835 – April 21, 1910

Twain

He believed that laughter was the
best elixir, that we were
better off chuckling
at the world's woes, and so
Tom Sawyer sallied
into my boyhood brio,
and I was more than half
in love with his lissome lass
and her pluck, and alone in the cloistered
quiet of my room, I dreamt
of Huck and Jim, adrift
on the Mississippi like a
pair of home-free hicks,
rafting into the hereafter
and hoisting their flag high.

D. H. Lawrence
September 11, 1885 – March 2, 1930

Lawrence

He penned novels of love
and its belonging, of our blood-
and-bone emotions, and one
steaming scene of a lady
and her lanky lover au
naturel, and I don't know
whether the tender public
was more vexed at the sex
or the hanky-panky between
a gamekeeper and his betters,
but whatever the case, fame
claimed him, and generations
of pimpled adolescents
got an itch for fiction.

Ernest Hemingway
July 21, 1899 – July 2, 1961

Hemingway

Your prose was as lean as a
willow unbent in the wind
and undisturbed by adverb
of phrase or cluttering clause,
and you loved the thrill of the bull
gored and the matador caressing it
with a cape, and the climax of the kill,
and your protagonists, ever pure
of heart, endured what they were
allotted with the gift of grace,
and like the old man
on the sea, fettered to a fish,
you bore the bruising of fame
and unlove until nothing
was left of life and wonderment,
and you took your gun and ended it.

John B. Lee
November 24th, 1951 –

Homage

I came late to your lissome
lyrics, that immaculate clamour
of sound and sense, the way
you tossed a lucid noose
over all things nude
in Nature and found a lexicon
suited to the fraught frantics
of our sexual awakening, words
to put the pith in pudendum
or the grr in groin, and a language
to limn your link to the land,
to the holies of the home ground,
to field and fallow, where a lad
could wander lonely and dream
in dactyls of the pristine passion
of poetry, or fancy a future
of love and laurels.

Don Gutteridge was born in Sarnia and raised in the nearby village of Point Edward. He taught High School English for seven years, later becoming a Professor in the Faculty of Education at Western University, where he is now Professor Emeritus. He is the author of more than seventy books: poetry, fiction and scholarly works in pedagogical theory and practice. He has published twenty-two novels, including the twelve-volume Marc Edwards mystery series, and forty books of poetry, one of which, Coppermine, was short-listed for the 1973 Governor-General's Award. In 1970 he won the UWO President's Medal for the best periodical poem of that year, "Death at Quebec." Don lives in London, Ontario.

Email: <u>dongutteridge37@gmail.com</u>.